*For Everything
A Season*

For Everything A Season

RALPH BAILEY

HAWTHORN BOOKS, INC.
W. *Clement Stone, Publisher*
NEW YORK

*To Vermelle, Kathy, and Bill—
personal partners for all seasons,
and the three greatest blessings
of my life*

Material from *The Eternal Now*, by Paul Tillich, reprinted by permission of Charles Scribner's Sons.
Material from *Markings*, by Dag Hammarskjöld, translated by Leif Sjoberg and W. H. Auden, reprinted by permission of the publisher. Copyright © 1964 by Alfred A. Knopf, Inc., and Faber and Faber Ltd.
Material from *Jonathan Livingston Seagull*, by Richard Bach, reprinted by permission of Macmillan Publishing Company, Inc. Text copyright © 1970 by Richard D. Bach.
Material from *The Prophet*, by Kahlil Gibran, reprinted with permission of the publisher, Alfred A. Knopf, Inc. Copyright 1923 by Kahlil Gibran; renewal copyright 1951 by Administrators C.T.A. of Kahlil Gibran Estate, and Mary G. Gibran.

FOR EVERYTHING A SEASON

Copyright © 1975 by Ralph Bailey. Copyright under International and Pan-American Copyright Conventions. All rights reserved, including the right to reproduce this book or portions thereof in any form, except for the inclusion of brief quotations in a review. All inquiries should be addressed to Hawthorn Books, Inc., 260 Madison Avenue, New York, New York 10016. This book was manufactured in the United States of America and published simultaneously in Canada by Prentice-Hall of Canada, Limited, 1870 Birchmount Road, Scarborough, Ontario.

Library of Congress Catalog Card Number: 75–2564
ISBN: 0–8015–2764–3
1 2 3 4 5 6 7 8 9 10

Contents

FOREWORD ix
PREFACE xiii
ACKNOWLEDGMENTS xv

Part I
A Time to Mourn

1 ANGELA 3
2 AFTERMATH 6
3 DOWN PAYMENT ON FUTILITY 10
4 DRIFTWOOD 12
5 I'D SAID IT, TOO . . . BUT SILENTLY 15
6 WHY? 16
7 THE HEADLINES AND THE WORLD CAME HOME 20
8 NEVER DREAMED SHE'D WRITE A DIFFERENT SCRIPT 22
9 WHAT HAPPENS WHEN YOUR LIFEBOAT LEAKS? 25

Part II
A Time to Dance

10 GOD SNEAKED IN THE BACK DOOR? 29
11 THE PICTURES CAME ALIVE 31
12 SORRY . . . WRONG NUMBER 34
13 KNOCK ME OVER WITH A FEATHER 37
14 ALMOST PERSUADED 39

CONTENTS

15	THE DIVINE PAYOFF	41
16	HAPPINESS AND HIGH HOPES	43
17	THE DAY THE SUPER SALESMAN CAME	45

Part III
A Time to Cast Away Stones

18	TUESDAY MORNING . . . 3:00 A.M.	49
19	MICHAEL	51
20	THE LONGEST NIGHT	53
21	SUNRISE SAW ME ON THE ROAD	55
22	WISH I DIDN'T HAVE TO TELL YOU	57
23	THE LONG RIDE HOME	59
24	ONE BABY BLANKET . . . BLUE	62

Part IV
A Time to Gather Stones Together

25	THE SONG SAID IT BEST	67
26	HE NEVER KNEW	69
27	PICK THEM UP	71
28	PUSH THEM OFF	73
29	KEEP THEM GOING	75
30	THE GIFT FROM MRS. BROWN	77

Part V
A Time to Seek

31	MOVE OUT	83
32	EVERYWHERE I GO . . . THERE I AM	85

CONTENTS

33	BALM IN GILEAD	86
34	SAW IT ON TV	88
35	AFTER TEN YEARS . . . WHY?	90
36	A NOT SO GENTLE REMINDER	92
37	THE NEW MOSES	94
38	A STRONG HAND AND A LITTLE LIGHT	96
39	LAST TAG	98

Foreword

Ralph Bailey is a winner. As the young set says, "This cat is together."

Authors see the works of aspiring writers by the mailbag full. And most of these are a drag. Reason? The average beginner is too much in a hurry. Plus, he hasn't reckoned the price of excellence.

For some months now I've been watching Ralph Bailey put these thoughts on paper. And I've come to admire his skill, plus his dedication to talk about agony in a helpful way.

As sure as we marry and have children, tragedy comes down the road to meet us. Never know for sure how, nor when. We only know one day it comes for sure.

So the secret obviously isn't to avoid hurt but to turn it into victory.

That's what the Baileys did.

I hope this book goes like terrific. What a Credo to give the sorrowing, the bleeding, the hurt. Because God is what he is, nobody knows for sure who will be blessed by what writer.

But I predict that Ralph Bailey will be a well-known name down the future in Christian literature. He writes with skill. He cuts right through the superficial to real issues. He keeps me reading. He convicts. He lifts.

And the Lord has always been looking for people like this.

CHARLIE SHEDD
Jekyll Island, Georgia

For everything there is a season,
and a time for every matter under heaven:
a time to be born, and a time to die;
a time to plant, and a time to pluck up
    what is planted;
a time to kill, and a time to heal;
a time to break down, and a time to build
    up;
a time to weep, and a time to laugh;
a time to mourn, and a time to dance;
a time to cast away stones, and a time
    to gather stones together;
a time to embrace, and a time to refrain
    from embracing;
a time to seek, and a time to lose;
a time to keep, and a time to cast away;
a time to rend, and a time to sew;
a time to keep silence, and a time to
    speak;
a time to love, and a time to hate,
a time for war, and a time for peace.

        Ecclesiastes 3:1–8   RSV

Preface

"For everything there is a season, and a time for every purpose under heaven."

True. And no one ever said it better than the writer of Ecclesiastes. He surveyed the human predicament and saw it whole. Weeping, laughing—mourning, dancing. They always are a package deal. We call it life.

Forget they go together and we're victimized by pride or pity. Remembering keeps us humble in our better days. Helps us off the canvas when we're floored. And sooner or later we all take a few punches. Sometimes it seems they'll never end.

The Psalmist knew the feeling:

"Has God forgotten to be gracious?"

Pure anguish. But he found a way around despair:

"I will remember."

So will I, Psalmist. You stood in darkness and remembered light. I'm standing in the sunshine. It threatens me to resurrect the feelings which I buried long ago. The gray days of the past cast shadows on me now . . . reach out to make the future less secure. But life goes on and so do I. Remembering . . . hoping.

I'll search for words I wish I'd heard back then. Test each sentence for validity. Listen for the solid ring of truth. No easy task. Sometimes nothing makes much sense, and words seem better left unsaid.

In my seasons of grief, some helps hindered:

Preachy pages turned me off.

Pie-in-the-sky ignored my present hunger.

FOR EVERYTHING A SEASON

How-to-do-it's had their place—before or after crisis. But during?

The best helpers had a rare capacity for acceptance. They never threw their verbal rocks at me when I felt low or tried to carve me in their image.

They understood, supported, encouraged me to look ahead. Taught me to remember.

I've waited ten years to tell my story. A long time on the road. And what have I to offer?

Simple answers to perplexing problems? No.

False hope? Forget it.

I've scanned my soul's horizon in a desperate search for hope. Occasionally I've found it. I'd like to tell you where and how. Give it to you straight. No phoniness.

In these intensely personal chapters I can share myself (something that I found along the way) . . . and I remember.

Acknowledgments

Thanks to the following super-people:

—Charlie and Martha Shedd. For their time, during which they gave me candid criticism, personal encouragement, and loving support, and for their profound influence on the life of my family. To Dr. Shedd, for being gracious enough to write a Foreword for this book.

—Evelyn Strickland. For time-out from a busy weekend to do a critical reading of the manuscript. Her suggestions were most helpful.

—Vermelle, my wife, for her willingness to rehash a particularly painful time of our lives and for allowing me to share with you some of our personal happenings. For typing and retyping page after page. For sharp editorial criticism mixed with a rare sense of humor. For her belief in the vital importance of telling this story. She pulled me through those hectic times when I wanted to throw in the towel and call it quits.

—My congregation, for allowing me the freedom to be my authentic self. For a duty-free month—enough time to complete the final draft.

PART I

A Time to Mourn

The literature of mankind is full of stories in which kings as well as beggars are reminded of their having to die. Man cannot stand the anticipation of death, and so he represses it. But the repression does not remove his ever present anxiety, and there are moments in the life of everyone when such repression is not even slightly effective. Then, we ask ourselves—will there be a time when I shall be forgotten, forever?

Paul Tillich, *The Eternal Now.* (New York: Charles Scribner's Sons, 1963), p. 33.

1
Angela

An hour after her birth, Angela died.

I ran from the hospital to the car. Sitting alone in the darkness, I propped my head against the steering wheel.

"Why?"

The reason went away with Angela.

༄

Blinding light . . . white blurr . . . nurse. Vermelle in and out of anesthesia's twilight zone.

"Have I had my baby?"

"Yes." No smile.

"Boy or girl?"

"Little girl."

"She O.K.?" No answer. "I said, is she O.K.?"

"The doctor'll talk to you in a few minutes."

Seemed more like hours, but he finally came. Green surgical suit, grim face, tired eyes.

"You're doing fine, just fine."

"And my baby?"

"Vermelle" . . . he wanted to console . . . "We did our best. I'm sorry." Silence as the truth explodes. "You're young. I hope you'll try again."

Try again. A softly spoken word. An open door to better days. But rebels running inner streets shouted down the quiet voice, an angry cry ringing in the emptiness; "We did our best. I'm sorry."

On my twenty-sixth birthday, I stood with friends beside the open grave.

"Here lies Angela." Our first child . . . a dream? Winter wind swept the cemetery and joined the gray sky in a colorless picture of my feelings.

The minister's words tore through mental numbness, falling hard against resentment's wall.

"Today, the wind blows as it has since time. Reminds us of God's eternity."

I thought of temporary things . . . like Angela, and happiness.

"Can't see him, but we feel his presence."

To me his absence seemed more real.

"Don't understand why such things happen . . . something good can come of it."

Hardly! I'd come to bury my birthday present!

"Tragedy turned to triumph at the cross."

"For whom?" I wondered. Certainly not for me.

The earth received Angela. I should have held her, snuggling, protecting from the cold, rewarded by her body next to mine.

In her room, Vermelle kept company with get-well cards

and gladiolas. Friends and nurses stopped by on their way to other things.

Silently, she sang the blues. I knew the lyrics: empty arms

2
Aftermath

Frail and weak, she sat, waiting. Waiting for the wheelchair that would take her to the car. She'd counted on a baby riding with her.
"Ready to go, Hon?" I hoped she'd smile.
"I don't know . . . don't care . . . not sure I'm ready."
"Sure you are. I've washed the dishes, emptied the garbage, the neighbors brought food. We won't have to cook for a week!"
"I'm not hungry."
Maybe I'd try another subject.
"Wow! I never saw so many flowers. We'll need a moving van!"
"Lousy substitute if you ask me."
Homecoming: A hundred times we'd let our minds race on to that great day. In our dreams we heard friends saying words new parents love to hear.
"Oh! What a precious baby."
"Isn't she a doll?"

AFTERMATH

"Looks exactly like her mother . . . or father . . . or both."
Should have been a gentle time. A chance for new beginnings. Instead it smashed us with a violent hand. I loved Vermelle, saw how much she'd hurt. That's why I'd packed up all the nursery items, removing everything that spoke of "Angela."

She stood, wavering in the doorway, hand against the wall for support. Sheer disbelief.

"What happened to the baby bed?"

. . . a gift from friends.

"The bassinette!"

. . . she'd used it as a child.

"The dresser!"

. . . with loving care we'd painted it and fixed it up with pictures.

She wept. Bitterly. I held her, choking back tears of my own.

"Honey, I tried to do the right thing."

The room: an echo chamber filled with one resounding voice . . .

"You are a loser! . . . Loser!! . . . LOSER!!!"

By afternoon the comforters came . . . bless them.

"Don't worry. Everything will be O.K. Remember" (hand on shoulder in a most confidential way) "time heals all wounds."

"Time? Damn time! . . . striking like a cobra in a corner . . . It's *now* we need help!"

༄

Her students were delighted when Vermelle returned to school.

"Hello, Mrs. Bailey, how's your baby?"

"Did you have a boy or a girl, Mrs. Bailey?"
"Hi, Mrs. Bailey. Glad you're back! Who's keeping your baby?"

※

Then those brutal telephone calls:
"Mrs. Bailey, this is Johnson's Pharmacy. We want to congratulate you on the birth of your daughter. We've a gift for her. Please stop by at your convenience."
Or:
"Is this Mrs. Bailey?"
"Yes."
"This is Mrs. Harris from the County Health Department. Over two months have passed since your baby came and she has no shot record. We hope you haven't forgotten to start her immunizations."

※

Frustration piled on frustration. Newborn infants reinforced our failure. We'd always loved them.
Conversations could begin with talk of politics or weather. Somehow they usually turned to children.
"Horace took his first step today."
"Little Mary can say, 'Da Da.'"
"Joe made the honor roll in school!"
Premarital pregnancy . . . always sorry when we heard . . . but now! And parents with unwanted children . . . what injustice!
Sometimes the morning paper told of child abuse. Misery with toast and coffee.
"If I were God I'd blast them from the face of the earth!"
We also hated ourselves and wondered if the poison

AFTERMATH

would spread until we despised each other. Arguments lasted long and ran hot. She asked why God would punish so severely; I wanted to forget the whole thing. When we'd reach a stalemate, I'd slam the door, leaving in a rage . . . running from something inside me.

Riding alone in the night, I'd search for a clue, a sign, anything pointing to a way from the confusion. I saw neon lights, empty streets, and darkness . . . and one drunk, staggering, on the way to nowhere. At least we had a common destination.

3
Down Payment on Futility

Topic: Furniture.
"Well . . . if you think we can afford it."
"I think we can afford it."
"I don't know . . . it's an awful lot of money."
"Honey," I reassured her, "when it comes to making you happy, money is no object. See, Vermelle, we're paying too much rent . . . you know we are."
"Right."
"Unfurnished would come cheaper."
"Right."
"So why not?"
"Why not?"
So much for the positive. We ignored the negative:
1. I would get a raise—in September, six months away.
2. We couldn't afford the down payment, either now or later.
3. We had no need for furniture. Wouldn't have for at

least five months, when we would return from a final summer of graduate school.

At the moment it made sense. Warped logic inspires sick decisions. With muddled minds and mixed motives, we dashed to the nearest store. Selected the furniture we'd often thought of buying . . . and made a down payment on futility. We thought we understood our rationale. A clear-cut case of "We-like-it-we'll-get-it." But hidden beneath a heap of shakey reasoning lived an ugly truth: We'd conned ourselves. Give her something else to think about and maybe she'd forget the baby.

Our number-one want: Angela. Next, a home of our own. With the first choice out of sight, we reached in frustration for the second.

"We'll buy the furniture now. Later, when it's paid for, we can get the house."

That's what we said. How we felt came closer to the truth: "Can't get a baby, but dammit, we'll get something."

A boobie prize to take the sting out of failure. New furniture only guaranteed we'd have a better place in which to cry.

There were bills to pay, schedules to meet. I remember saying on a desperate day, "We can't afford to sit and rot. We can't give up, but, Lord, how I'd like to . . ."

Life rushed on . . . never had a chance to catch our breath.

4
Driftwood

Driftwood—twisted, distorted, sun-bleached. Punished by the pounding waves. Captive of the currents. Swept along until (if luck holds out) it finds the way to some deserted beach (beaches beat the mud flats every time). Settles in the snow white sands and waits . . . until another high tide comes or lovers look for firewood or someone picks it up and takes it home.

Driftwood: nice to see—hell to be. If wood had feelings, we'd be brothers.

Floating, no direction, destination unknown. Subject to to the whims of wind and water.

Helpless . . . a storm comes to the sea of life, you take a beating.

DRIFTWOOD

Grief . . . the pain of separation. Dislodged from people, places, things that give us life. Agonizing. Especially during those sleepless nights that seemed to have no end.

Resentment . . . a poison. We had our share.
"What in the name of God have we done to deserve such treatment?"

Bitterness . . . the friendly helpers on the shore would tip their hat in our direction. Run along the bank and shout encouragement.
"Have faith. Trust in God . . . He'll guide you all the way."
Who wants guidance on a trip you didn't choose? We'd mumble a reply, "After all he's done for me! . . . I can hardly wait."
Some pitched clichés on God and hope. Others tossed verbal sugar sticks and hollow phrases wrapped in false assurance.
Advice—cheap. And we weren't taking.
"Remember. When the going gets tough, the tough get going."
"Who is tough in times like these?"
People acted so secure. With the corners of their faith nailed down, they surely couldn't understand. The rage, the fear, the anxiety . . . all belonged to us. Or so we thought.
They spoke of inner peace as part of Christian living. We fought our private war and felt the extra weight of guilt for being different.
Occasionally we'd meet a fellow struggler. Beaten on a dozen different beachheads, scarred, weathered, still moving

on. One phrase from them meant more than fancy sermons from the rest.

"I've been there."

Magic words from no-man's land to lend a sense of credibility. They spoke. We felt a healing touch.

"It helps to tune in to your feelings. Share what's going on inside."

"If you knew what we felt, you wouldn't ask to hear it."

We'd shed a tear. They'd comfort us and cry a little, too.

"You can't shock me. I've said it all or thought it. You can't surprise God. He knows the score. And you can't fool yourself. So why not?"

Made more sense than anything we'd heard. Brought relief if only for the moment.

Eventually we learned to ride the tide. Before we did, we saw some devastating sights.

Family functions—torture. Reminded us of what we'd lost. Special days (Mother's Day, Father's Day, etc.)— creeping hells. Drawing nearer until they'd pass and circle back to come again.

We wondered, Will it take forty years to find the promised land where time heals wounds and God is love?

5
I'd Said It, Too ... But Silently

She stared from the bedroom window. A rope hung from a tree in our backyard. The noose; a pendulum, back and forth, moved by gentle breeze . . . signs there'd been a child at play—but not our child.
"Vermelle, I'm home . . . Vermelle! . . . Vermelle!!"
"Huh . . . what?"
"What *are* you doing?"
"Thinking . . . just thinking, that's all."
"What about?"
"Nothing in particular."
"I know *something's* on your mind. I called three times."
She turned. Bitter fire dancing in her eyes. "I'm thinking I would rather die than live."
"Stop it! You can't say that!"
I'd said it, too. But always silently.

6
Why?

The minister braced himself against the pulpit (elegant before a wall of floral tributes), glanced across the saddened congregation, and began.

"God looked down from heaven last Thursday . . . viewed the lovely flowers blooming in his garden."

A baby's funeral at a neighborhood church.

"Found the most perfect rosebud . . . picked it to beautify his house."

God, acting on Divine whim, snatching babies from their parents to make his house more attractive. Totally unbelievable and repulsive.

I exploded with anger. Had the urge to shout him down or punch him in the nose or leave. Instead, I sat. Fuming.

But the question bubbled to the top . . . it always did. Yeast for endless fermentation.

"Why?"

Haunting, distracting, frustrating.

In the middle of a movie.

WHY?

At work.
In bed.
At a party.
"Why?"
Consistently unanswered.

We studied ... books, tracts, articles sent by friends, anything to help us understand. A statement caught our eye. We weighed it. Tested every phase for sensibility. Wondered if the author knew his stuff. Expected that he wouldn't. After all the reading the question still remained. "Why?"

We longed for solid answers that could satisfy our need to know ... and mired in a bog of possibility.

1. *Suppose there is no God?*

Then life becomes a cruel trick. Played by fools so insecure they search for order even in the midst of chaos. We almost took a cut at that idea, but Divine signs popped up here and there.

Human life—too wonderful for chance. During the pregnancy we had had occasion to watch a miracle unfold. The conception, growth, birth of a baby—special gifts from God.

"Put your hand right here and you can feel the baby kick ... there ... feel it?" Accidental death I could believe. But accidental life? Impossible.

A starry night ... the awe-inspiring quality of infinity.

The beauty of the heavens. The orderliness of the universe spoke of a Master Maker. We affirmed the presence of a God behind the process of creation.

The church . . . a testimony in itself. At a given point in time something happened to a small group of men. Changed their life-style in a most dramatic way. The resurrection of Jesus Christ brought them out of hiding . . . endowed them with new boldness. Set them on a path that shaped our history. Exactly what happened on the first Easter is academically debatable. *That* some profound event took place is certain. The church reminded us that twelve men, convinced of what they'd seen, bet their lives on God's continued presence.

Stalemate: End of argument.

"O.K. I give up. It's irrational to disbelieve in God. Then why did he let my baby die?"

2. *Maybe he prefers noninvolvement in human affairs.*

Considered, but rejected. Creation appears continuous. Hard to believe in a God who made the world, then stepped out of the picture. Every creator has continued interest in his product. Jesus of Nazareth—God's Son—the ultimate expression of Divine involvement with humanity.

3. *Perhaps God punished us.*

Scripture can be problematic when used to find right answers in improper places.

"The righteous will be fruitful and multiply. What's wrong with me? What have I done?"

"Nothing!" I'd heard enough to last me for awhile. "Can't you get it through your head?"

Mac, a friend with a special way of saying things, put it like this.

"God does pay off, but not every Saturday night."

"Then, why? Why?"

I wondered if we'd ever know. Heaven's window had closed curtains.

7
The Headlines and the World Came Home

"You've been in a tailspin long enough," our minister reminded us one evening. "You've had a tough time, but so have others." And he named a few. "They all recovered. Isn't it time you made a move?"

Good point. But Vermelle disliked being jabbed with it. She struck back.

"Isn't it time you made a move? . . . like out of my house. And don't bother to come again."

Hate God, hate his man.

Like it or not, he'd hit us with a truth: Returning to the human race is both painful and necessary. He also raised an important question. Why had a comparatively minor tragedy done so much damage to our lives?

Others *had* regained their balance. Why couldn't we? The answer . . . buried deep beneath the rubble. We'd lost more than a baby.

THE HEADLINES AND THE WORLD CAME HOME

Tragedy: something terribly unpleasant that affected others. We read the headlines:
"Plane Crash Kills 80."
"Volcano Erupts Destroying Entire Town."
"Multi-car Smash-up Leaves Six Dead."
Happened every day . . . but not to us. We thought in terms of immortality, occupied ourselves with living, took a casual view of death.

"Why worry? We've all got to go sooner or later. When he calls, I'll come, and not a minute before."

"Only two things certain—death and taxes."

I'd made acquaintance with taxes. Death I hadn't met. After our first encounter I saw through different glasses.

A new set of questions came to mind.

"Is everything we've struggled for so easily lost?"

"What is important?"

"With our value system broken down, where and in what can we find a sense of personal worth?"

One day thoughts drifted back to Thomas. On a sleepy eighth-grade afternoon, he had cried . . . no apparent reason . . . sobs; the only sound in study hall. The teacher asked him why.

"I just realized something. One day I'm gonna have to die."

Funny back then, but after Angela, I quit laughing.

The headlines and the world came home. I grieved for lost security—the bliss of ignorance.

8
Never Dreamed She'd Write a Different Script

In retrospect, I see more clearly. Our life-style added to the load of grief and blocked the healing process. Couldn't get over Angela until we learned to get around ourselves.

Example? Try this conversation from the past. We were: (a) recently married (b) new in town (c) beginning the first job after college (d) looking for a place in which to worship. Went like this:

"You're planning to join the Methodist Church?"
"Yes."
"Then you should come with us."
Loved the warmth of feeling wanted.
"You'll come in contact with the 'best' people."
Instant status—irresistible.
"Make connections that could be an asset in your work."
More enticing every minute.

NEVER DREAMED SHE'D WRITE A DIFFERENT SCRIPT

"May as well make the most of your church affiliation." Sadly, I confess, what he said made sense. Part two added frosting on the cake.

"You may want to join the choir. Know you enjoy music . . . and, up there, they never take an offering."

One question pulled the trigger on our decision. Which church would best blend worship with the pursuit of success?

We found the place . . . signed on the dotted line. Case closed. Never heard of losing self in service, of the joy it brings. We missed the big idea until we moved to a less exclusive congregation for a different set of reasons.

Fear of failure tied us down and stifled creativity. We had two general rules:

1. Never take a risk.
2. Stick to what is tried and proven.

With limited alternatives we found life boring. Nothing satisfied.

Angela symbolized marital success, an area where no one wants to fail. Naturally we'd programmed her to fit our unrealistic model of the happy life.

She'd look exactly as we planned. Blue eyes, curly hair. She'd hardly ever cry, and if she did, we'd know precisely how to make her stop. Ideal parents with a lovely child.

Of course she'd be obedient. Unruly children, showing off in public places bring embarrassment to parents. Self-image couldn't stand the threat.

An adolescent without rebellion.

A young adult who (after winning a beauty contest and graduating from an impressive university) would marry the ideal guy. Settle down to raise a lovely family.

FOR EVERYTHING A SEASON

All in all she'd make us very proud. We had the drama ready for production. Never dreamed she'd write a different script.

But she did. And we'd have gladly swapped our fancy hopes for the privilege of standing on the stage with her ... while she did her own act.

9

What Happens When Your Lifeboat Leaks?

What happens when your lifeboat leaks? Pressing question when you've come to feel at home in it. We had.

Our faith fit like an old shoe: nice and comfortable. We'd planned on riding it through life and death. Suddenly came unglued. Bad news. On the shore; seemed secure enough. In the water . . . quite another story. Did people play religious games to pacify themselves?

We'd think about it later. For now, we had other problems . . . like, what happens when your lifeboat leaks? We found three alternatives:

1. Pretend nothing happened. Business as usual. Keep the faith and overlook the contradictions. Talk a good game . . . raise your voice to further hide the insecurity. Make pompous remarks to reassure yourself.

"I'm as good as the next man."

Keep smiling. No one knows you're sinking until you go down.

2. Abandon ship. A choice we didn't have. Broken people lack the stamina for swimming or for searching out new modes of transportation.

3. Stay with it in spite of shortcomings. Row like crazy ... bail as if your life depended on it (which it does). Hoping against hope that somehow, somewhere, if you hang in there long enough, help will come.

We chose the latter. Partly because of it's familiarity, partly because we didn't know where to look for a more fulfilling faith, partly because we knew, more than ever, how much we needed a power greater than ourselves.

PART II

A Time to Dance

I don't know who—or what—put the question, I don't know when it was put. I don't even remember answering. But at some moment I did answer *yes* to Someone—or something—and from that hour I was certain that existence is meaningful and that, therefore, my life, in self-surrender, had a goal.

Dag Hammarskjöld. *Markings*. (New York: Alfred A. Knopf, 1964), p. 205.

10
God Sneaked in the Back Door?

God sneaked in the back door. At least it seems he did. It's possible he never left . . . and in those moments when his absence seemed so real, I may have closed my door on him. In bitterness we missed so many signs that could have changed our course.

I remember leaving the delivery room on the night Angela died. The doctor took me there to see her body. I couldn't cry. Senses numbed by shock. Came through swinging doors and met a dozen friends from church, standing in the hall. They'd come to celebrate.

Tears welled up. Words wouldn't come. Shook my head. "No!" Ran . . . through the group of people . . . along the corridor . . . down the winding stairway . . . out the fire exit. On my way to personal despair, I passed straight through the Christian fellowship—and never even noticed.

Or in the parking lot: alone . . . until I felt an arm around my shoulder. Heard the quiet sob of someone crying with me. A friend's sorrow—symbol of God's grief?

FOR EVERYTHING A SEASON

At home: the empty house seemed overbearing. Depressed. Alone. Loaded with doubt. Calling to the powers-that-be for help in my disaster area. Wondering if a God existed.

"Help me!"

Over and over. Kneeling by my bed.

"Help me!"

Suddenly I felt a surge of power in the wasteland of my life.

"And the earth was without form and void. And the Spirit of God moved across the face of the deep."

Creating . . . making all things new. But somehow in the rush of circumstances, I forgot. The turmoil of the next few weeks drove healing thoughts into a wilderness.

God sneaked in the back door? I'm not sure how or when he entered. I only know the sun came up and brought along a ray of hope. I hurried out of bed, admired the beginning of a beautiful day, noticed the parade of life had passed.

No point in standing on the corner all alone. Thought I'd march awhile. Ran to find my place. Hoping I could still catch up with the procession.

The back door? Maybe—but more than likely I left him . . . standing in a corridor . . . in a parking lot . . . or in any of a thousand places I'd felt alone and lost.

11
The Pictures Came Alive

In a vivid panorama the pictures came alive:
  Arrest and trial of Jesus.
  Calvary.
  Crucifixion.
  Cross.
  Suffering.
  Resurrection.
  All my life I'd heard the words—but never so completely. This year people stepped from musty Bible pages. Sermonic words fell with the solid sound of steel on steel.
  "And he stood before Pontius Pilate . . . accused."
  Rotten deal.
  "They slapped him . . . cursed him . . . spit in his face . . . pressed a crown of thorns on his head."
  Saw myself among the vicious crowd.
  "Totally rejected by the ones he loved."
  And by those of us who'd ignored him. I felt the sting of guilt.

"Made him bear the burden of his cross. Followed down Jerusalem's dusty streets and watched him fall beneath the load, even as we crumpled under ours."

One day in basic training, I'd collapsed from too much running. Lay face down in the dirt while four platoons ran over and around me on the way to supper, but nothing ever pushed my face into the ground like Angela.

"And when they came to a place called Calvary, they crucified him."

I cringed with every hammer blow. Nails ripping human flesh. Excruciating pain, loneliness, humiliation, the sense of failure. The desperation of a man forsaken by his Father.

"But God was there at Calvary."

. . . Then he was present in my grief.

"And he loved his Son and hurt with him . . . and he hurts for us today."

The suffering, the mental anguish, the helplessness of his friends and family who watched, the burden on the heart of God. Somehow it seemed that because God dared to suffer, he could better understand our problems.

I'd missed the meaning of the agony of God until I realized he agonized for me.

Good Friday lived—and maybe for the first time so did I. Flash of insight: If God sent his Son to Calvary for me . . . then I'm important . . . I matter . . . I have worth . . . I am a success.

I relaxed. Free to risk, knowing that if God could redeem a failure like the cross, he could also handle mine. In those days I felt a growing sensitivity . . . settling quietly . . . a night fog blowing in from sea.

The cross spoke loud and clear.

"I am for you."

Best news I'd ever heard. A cool drink of water in the heat of turmoil.

God lost a Son, we lost a daughter. He gave his. We clung possessively to ours.

12
Sorry ... Wrong Number

"Sorry . . . wrong number."
Disinterested response to the silent voice, speaking from a quiet corner of my mental storehouse, as an old idea emerged. One I'd dealt with years before.
"I need you."
"Sorry . . . wrong number. Please consult your directory or dial information."
Emotions get confused in the aftermath of tragedy. Can't afford to act on impulse.
"I need you."
"Sorry, wrong number!"
The ministry; I'd considered . . . (a terrible idea after being turned off by the stereotypes) . . . gave it up, and went the other way. When I least expected, it returned to wash me in a wave of decision.
"I need you."
Vermelle and I agreed we'd always share our problems. No need to fight those personal struggles single-handed.

"Which," I pondered, "is the lesser of the two evils—battling alone or opening my heart to her?"

She still blamed God for taking Angela. She'd worked to help me through graduate school. I promised, "When this year is over, we will settle down." Suggest we quit our jobs . . . begin again?

"Not on a bet!"

But it got the best of me. The notion swirled around inside. Demanded to be put into words.

"Honey, I think you'd better sit down."

"Sit down? Whatever for?"

"Something I've got to tell you."

Fear and curiosity. With all the ceremony, she expected the worst.

"Vermelle, what would you say if I . . . well . . . now, don't think I'm crazy . . . but, I think I'm wanted in the ministry."

Silence . . . seemed like minutes. When she spoke, her words were cool and even. Mechanical with no emotion.

"After what he did . . . he wouldn't want us . . . would he?"

"Honey, I'm not at all sure . . . But . . . suppose he does? What then?"

She thought a moment. "I guess we'd have to follow. If we didn't . . . and he really called . . . he'd punish even worse."

"Can't you understand he doesn't punish?"

Not convinced, but at least she listened.

"If he says go, we'll pack our things. But you be sure, you be damned sure."

I took her hand. "Promise, nothing drastic until I'm certain."

Days passed with no assurance. In the doldrums; waiting for a breeze to move us—in any direction.

"Am I the kind of fool," I wondered, "who enjoys the state of inner turmoil?"

13
Knock Me Over With a Feather

On Easter Eve, a little before midnight, I made my conditional decision . . . "I will, if."

"If you insist, I'll go . . . but I can't afford a wild-goose chase. Vermelle has suffered too much. I'll go, but not unless I'm positive. Give me a sign . . . something I can't miss . . . and before the weekend is over. If you want me, say so!"

Immediately the tension I'd been feeling disappeared, replaced by an overwhelming sense of peace.

"Get up. Go to your Bible. Read the tenth chapter of Matthew, verse seven." No voice from heaven, but a gentle wave of inspiration.

I *did* ask for a sign. Opening the Book, I leafed hurriedly through the pages.

Chapter sixteen . . . fifteen . . . fourteen . . . thirteen . . . and the parable of the sower caught my eye.

"Other seeds fell upon thorns, and the thorns grew up and choked them."

The story of my life. Nothing wrong with seed or soil.

But trivia had grown like weeds to strangle life. Regardless of the decision, there'd be some changes made. Curiosity pushed me on.

Chapter ten: Ran my finger up the page until I found the verse. Could have knocked me over with a feather!

"And as you go, preach."

I'm a stubborn man, not subject to be moved by chance. I wasn't sure. We talked it over . . . couldn't sleep . . . took a midnight ride and sorted through the questions as they popped into our heads.

"Did I know the verse?" . . .

Not consciously.

"ESP or something similar?"

Possible.

"A simple coincidence."

Maybe.

In the church a light still burned. The pastor's study.

"Bill, we've got to talk to you." Told him everything. "Could it be a sign?"

"Could be . . . but it's your decision. Some things are between a man and God. This is one match you'll have to fight alone."

Easter morning; the sun rose bright . . . inside and out. We kept the happenings in our hearts, still uncertain.

14

Almost Persuaded

My attention kept escaping through the sanctuary walls . . . roamed around outside.
"I hope the guy who invented Evening Worship suffered an early transmission failure . . . in the rush-hour traffic."
I held a handful of valid reasons for staying home.
"Too tired."
"Rather watch TV."
"Tough week ahead, etc."
Reluctantly, I ambled over to the weekly exercise in self-discipline.
"Anything I so actively begrudge . . . must be good for me."
Sang the hymns . . . with something less than a "joyful" noise.
"If we stand again, I'll scream!"
Then Carlos did his thing . . . a solo.
"Almost Persuaded." The words hit home and gathered up my scattered thoughts.

I'd "almost" done so many things. Squeaked by . . . getting the job done, but just barely. Total commitment: no specialty of mine.

"Almost Persuaded."

The final words crashed into my complacency: "Almost, is lost." The artillery did the softening, and the infantry moved in for the kill.

I'll forever remember the sermon—about the rich man coming to Jesus with a question.

"What must I do?"

I'd asked a hundred times in the last few weeks.

The answer: Too much . . . "Sell everything."

"When the young man heard this, he went away sorrowfully."

"Almost Persuaded."

Church over. I rushed Vermelle outside.

"Honey, remember what we said? . . . 'Nothing drastic until I'm positive.' "

"I remember."

"Well . . . we'd better get our business affairs in order."

With that, my war ended . . . "Not with a bang," as the saying goes, "but with a whimper."

15

The Divine Payoff

I'd signed the peace treaty, but Vermelle still fought. Clearly and concisely, she drew her battle lines.

"Listen, God . . . you're asking us to pull up stakes and start all over. I'll do it, but only if, before we go, you give us another baby."

Under those uncompromising terms, we existed. I finished school and taught a year to meet financial obligations. (And to see if something else might happen to make me change my mind.) She waited for the Divine payoff.

Another baby: the solution to her problem. But weeks and months went by, and disappointment was the only thing conceived.

The doctor sounded sure of his prescription. "Relax, Vermelle. Quit worrying. There's not a reason in the world why you can't get pregnant."

"How in the name of heaven do you relax when you so desperately want a baby? . . . And quit worrying? . . . Impossible!"

FOR EVERYTHING A SEASON

Almost a year passed, and we'd begun to wonder.

No baby! Time running out. Apparently, we wouldn't meet her deadline. Vermelle threw in the towel.
"O.K., God. I surrender. Whatever you want, I'll do it."
Peace at last.

One night during supper, she raised a question.
"Have you ever thought we might adopt?"
I had. Almost daily for the last three months.
"Do you think we could?"
"Why not? First thing in the morning we'll schedule an interview."
Long time since I'd seen so radiant a smile.
The first appointment with the agency: mostly routine. An overview of the process, probable length of waiting period, list of things required of us, information forms to fill out and return. Not much, but it made her very happy.
"At last . . . we're finally on the move."
Never went back for the second meeting. Morning sickness. She rushed home from a visit with her doctor. Ecstatic.
"Suspicion confirmed! We're going to have a baby!!"

16
Happiness and High Hopes

Happiness and high hopes. Beautiful!
Days filled with necessary chores in preparation for a new beginning:
A visit to the university.
Job hunting.
Search for an apartment to fit a student's budget.
Sell the furniture—the sorry substitute we'd used when all else failed.
Pay the bills.

Zero hour: Mixed emotions, sad good-byes, a few tears. But deep inside, an assurance.
"You're doing the right thing."

Doors opened as if by magic. The pieces fell in place.
Registration day: "Report to the Emory Field House . . .

FOR EVERYTHING A SEASON

9:00 A.M." Long lines and short tempers. But not for me. I signed my name on course rolls. Paid my fees. Floated down the sidewalk on cloud nine.

Came home happy.

"Honey, I was made for this!"

※

I lost myself in study, and we waited. Counted days and months. Each passing week left in its wake new confidence.

"The second time around, there'd be no hitches."

Visits to the doctor consistently brought good news.

"All systems: Go! T-minus two months and counting."

Angela had come a few weeks early. After passing that milestone, we had a celebration—steaks, and a night on the town.

Nearing the target date, time . . . which had been flying . . . began to crawl.

17
The Day the Super Salesman Came

He walked into our living room as if he owned the house. Spreading his sample case across our sofa, the super salesman made his pitch.

"Sir, one of the most treasured possessions a couple can own is a pictorial record of a child's growth."

Obviously we'd have something to photograph shortly.

"Children grow so rapidly. Our plan is the best there is. Absolutely incomparable. Nine beautiful photos, taken at two-month intervals . . . and only sixty dollars. Plus . . . at no extra cost . . . this lovely album, itself worth more than fifteen dollars. Isn't it gorgeous, Mrs. Bailey?"

Had to say yes.

"Remember, Mr. and Mrs. Bailey, you can't recapture those marvelous days of childhood development. Once they're past . . . gone forever."

He almost made a sale . . . but not quite.

FOR EVERYTHING A SEASON

"Think we'd better wait."

"Wait? Mr. Bailey, don't make a mistake you'd regret the rest of your life. I might not come to this territory again."

"Guess I'll have to take my chances."

"I wish you'd give me one good reason——"

"We'd have a hard time paying for it now——"

"The question, Mr. and Mrs. Bailey is not, 'Can I afford it.' Rather you should ask, 'Can I afford to be without it?'"

"Look . . . we lost our first child. Don't want to count on anything too soon. We'd rather wait."

"Craziest thing I ever heard." Grabbed his briefcase, slammed it shut, stalked out in a huff, mumbling. "Absolutely the craziest thing I've ever heard! . . . Sorry I wasted both your time and mine."

Made me mad . . . but he also made me think.

"Suppose something did go wrong. Could we stand it a second time?"

Nine months passed. No action.

Two weeks later, and we assured ourselves. "Every day a better chance of success."

We enjoyed the jokes . . . about riding over rough roads and railroad tracks to help Mother Nature do her work.

PART III

A Time to Cast Away Stones

BRAND (his face lifted up towards the descending avalanche):
   The jaws of death encompass me
   God above!
   Does it all count for naught with Thee
   That man in anguish strives to be?
(The avalanche sweeps him away. The valley is buried in snow. Through the roar a Voice is heard.)

VOICE: God is love.

   Ibsen: *Brand*, trans. W. H. Auden, in Dag Hammarskjöld, *Markings*. (New York: Alfred A. Knopf, 1964), p. 204.

18
Tuesday Morning . . . 3:00 A.M.

Tuesday morning. 3:00 A.M. Wife speaking.
"Honey, let's go to the hospital."
I jumped out of bed, wide awake. We'd spoken of it often. Silently, we'd hoped . . . the World Series and Super Bowl rolled into one!
We dressed . . . sat holding hands . . . quiet, except for the perking coffee pot whose incense filled the room.
The moment: a profound time demanding a religious response. We thanked God for setting up the game plan and invited him into our day.
Devotional guide . . . November 10th, 1964. I read:
"So you have sorrow now, but I will see you again." (John 16:22b)
Can't remember getting past the scripture. Fear crossed her face like a cloud covering the sun. She looked at something no one else could see.
"Only a coincidence. Don't worry," and I laughed to hide uneasiness.

"Maybe he's telling us something."

"Could be" . . . thinking fast . . . "It's reassurance. We've had our share of disappointment. Now's the time for happiness." I smiled, but inside the string tightened.

Headlights cut the mist and reached out to stab the night. Windshield wipers rhythmically pushed aside a melting coat of frost. We were warm.

In the parking lot, we prayed. I kissed her one last time.

Cold wind came in the open door, chasing security and warmth. No turning back.

19

Michael

Nine hours later, I met Michael, a squirming bundle held for my inspection. Three ways he differed from his cradle colleagues: more red, more wrinkles, and more volume.

"Man, I'm glad that's over" . . . a sigh of relief . . . "If I could just see Vermelle . . . but at least we're ahead at half-time."

I worried when an hour passed with no word from recovery. Frantic when I hadn't heard in two.

"What about my wife?" I asked a tired lady armed with a pint of plasma.

"Can't talk now." Tossed over her shoulder as she disappeared through the swinging doors.

👑

The doctor *could* talk. He shot straight.

"Ralph, she's having a problem. Bleeding badly . . . we can't seem to stop it. We're doing all we can. I'll keep you posted."

👑

FOR EVERYTHING A SEASON

That's when Bill and Jean came . . . they always do. They'd driven miles to bring a potted plant and say, "I care." Without them, the next grim bulletin might have been too much to bear.

"The blood bank's out of her type. Sent the state police for more, but we can't wait. I'd like to transfer her to Emory."

"Please hurry!" . . . an afterthought, "Can I ride with her?"

"No!" . . . then more softly, "That wouldn't be best."

Wailing siren.
    Speeding ambulance.
        Red light flashing in the dusk.
            A horror story.

Snellville: Car ignored the warning . . . eased into the intersection. Near collision.

Stone Mountain: "Atlanta—16 miles" . . . blood pressure falling fast . . . no pulse . . . "We're going to lose her!"

Emory University Hospital: Blood pressure 0/0 . . . in shock.

Driver to physician, "Do you think they're ready upstairs?"

"We're coming, ready or not."

From the open door light spilled into the darkness and splashed across her face. Deathly pale . . . unconscious . . . eyes rolled . . . oxygen mask . . . every breath, a dying gasp at life itself.

"Get her admitted!" the doctor ordered when he noticed me. Hurriedly, they wheeled her out of sight.

52

20

The Longest Night

"You'll have to wait your turn."

She resented being interrupted. They're always busy in admissions. I wasn't in the mood for waiting, or for middle names and numbers. So I left her with insurance forms and blanks to fill with vital information.

Upstairs, I walked and worried and, in between, gave thanks for friends who'd come two hundred miles.

Occasional reports from surgery kept me going . . . hoping . . . small windows in a wall that shut me out.

"We're going to do a hysterectomy . . . the only way to save her."

"Still hanging on . . . a real fighter."

"Vital signs stabilizing."

After five hours: "They've stopped the bleeding. Closing the incision now."

"She's in recovery."

"I want to be honest with you. Two more minutes and she'd have been dead on arrival. Had to give her ten pints of blood. It'll take five days to know what to expect. All we can do now is wait . . . hope for the best. Why not get some rest and come back tomorrow?"

Tomorrow seemed forever. Fiendish nightmares punctuated troubled sleep. They had a common theme.

I'd known what to do with Angela, but what do you do with a day-old baby . . . if his mother dies?

21
Sunrise Saw Me on the Road

Sunrise saw me on the road. Going home. No need to waste a morning waiting in Atlanta. Visiting hours in intensive care didn't start until eleven; besides I needed reassurance. Had to see Michael.

Walton County Hospital: face against the showroom glass. (A child at the window of the candy store?)

"That's my boy! King of the nursery."

I hurried home to shave and shower. Packed a few clothes . . . grabbed a sandwich.

"How long's it been? My last meal seems like ancient history."

Yesterday did a mental rerun. Worse the second time around.

Back to Atlanta: For forty miles I played mind games. Remembering how she looked last night. Wondering what I'd see this morning. Trying all the possibilities for size. Frightened . . . could she read the feeling in my face? Would she even be aware I'd come?

FOR EVERYTHING A SEASON

I parked. Walked slowly to the hospital. Took an elevator . . . glad, for once, it stopped at every floor.

"Intensive Care. Please Knock." I knocked.

"Pardon me, ma'am. I'm Ralph Bailey. My wife . . . you've got her in there. I know it's not quite eleven, but——"

"Of course, Mr. Bailey. Come right in."

I opened her door . . . fearfully (afraid to ask her condition) . . . braced for whatever.

Total surprise: Sitting up in bed, she'd combed her hair . . . putting on makeup. She opened fire.

"Where the devil have you been all day! Waited since six this morning!"

Mad, but I loved the spirit.

"You should see your son!"

Anger disappeared.

"Is he O.K.?"

"Sure."

"Thank God! They said he was, but I didn't know whether to believe them."

"He's looking great."

"You're not kidding?"

"Honey! About that? There's only one thing."

"What?"

"He needs you."

Smiling. "Tell him he can count on it."

22
Wish I Didn't Have to Tell You

Wednesday . . . I'll never forget it. After a week in the hospital, Vermelle was going home (amazing recovery). And, for the first time, I held Michael. Wrapped him in a blanket, getting ready for his introduction to the great outdoors.

"Gosh, babies are heavy . . . and wiggly."

"Relax, Mr. Bailey, they're hard to break."

I took the formula the nurse had made . . . "Very important. Never go anywhere without it."

Disposable diapers . . . "They're important, too, as you'll see in a few minutes."

"Heavens! What'll I do?"

Off we went to Emory.

Baby meets mother: Some reunion! I wish you could have seen it. The next few days: the kind you read about in books, but hardly ever come to know. Feelings, denied too long, came up to celebrate. Friends stopped by in droves to bring best wishes and to share our joy.

I had a son—and a resurrected wife—for which to give thanks. On Friday, I went to church. Seminary worship at Emory's Durham Chapel.
Prelude.
Call to Worship.
Hymn of Praise.
Tap on the shoulder.
Shattered reverie.
Whispered. "There's a message for you."
Annoyed. "Can't it wait?"
"Better come now. They say it's urgent."
I hurried across the street to the student affairs office.
"Come in, Ralph."
The secretary stood, propping herself against the desk to keep from falling. On her face a most pathetic look that melted in a burst of tears.
"Ralph, I'm afraid I've got bad news——"
. . . between sobs . . . "Wish I didn't have to tell you . . .
. . . Your son just died."

23
The Long Ride Home

The hills of North Georgia: how I loved them—but on the long ride home I cursed each one for standing in my way. (Miles stretch on forever when you ride them with a broken heart.) The old car sputtered and complained at being pushed too hard. My outer shell remained intact . . . inside I turned to jelly.

To myself: "Dammit, John, please hurry! Of all the days to have come in someone else's car!"

Slowly, up every incline . . . inching our way to the top . . . coasting down the other side . . . hope rising with the speed . . . squelched by yet another hill.

My mind ran freely . . . up and down the highway. To Atlanta: reliving the moment when I heard the news. Remembering the words of a friend:

"I don't know why this happened." At least an honest start . . . something I appreciated. "Maybe there are special children who need to blend their personality with your uniqueness. You might never discover them if you had

FOR EVERYTHING A SEASON

your own. Keep looking. One day . . . in the bullrushes . . . you may find a new Moses."

To home: worrying . . . wondering . . . wanting to disbelieve the message I had received. Reviewing the possibilities:

Vermelle smiling at the door: "Hi . . . missed you . . . and I'm glad you're home."

Impossible.

Or: In the rocker . . . holding Michael while he slept.

A fantasy.

Maybe I'd find Michael sound asleep in bed.

Stupid thoughts. More than likely I would find the worst.

Vermelle . . . in my mind I saw her overcome with despair. Painted in a hundred different shades of grief. Could she stand the strain? I wondered as the miles dragged on and on.

"John, go faster."

"Running wide open."

"Wide open at fifty-five? Oh Boy! I could run faster."

Before the car had fully stopped, I opened the door, jumped out, flew down the walk. Into the house. I knew I'd heard the right report.

Michael died. Through the tears she told me how:

"Just quit breathing!"

"No!"

"Right here beside me in the bed . . . thought he'd gone to sleep. Never even cried! Asked Peggy to move him . . . and he wasn't breathing."

"And then you called the doctor?"

"He came. Tried everything . . . but too late."

In one of those moments when an embrace says more than words, we held each other tight. And cried until we couldn't.

24

One Baby Blanket . . . Blue

"One baby blanket . . . blue."
Neatly catalogued among the gifts received when we expected Angela. Stored with all the other things after she had died. Brought out again to use with Michael.
"One baby blanket."
Soft to the touch. Spiced with the scent of oil and powder. Speaking of new life.
Earlier in the morning as I left, I kissed him lightly as he slept . . . tucked him in so he could rest a little longer. Should have waked him, because I'd never have another chance.
Baby blankets and death are contradictions. Pulled it back so I could see his face. Armies of feeling converged from every corner of my soul. Clashed in fierce combat. I wished they'd find another battlefield.
In a little while the men would come for Michael. I covered him . . . turned . . . walked away.
In the bedroom, I knelt . . . took her hand

ONE BABY BLANKET . . . BLUE

"Vermelle, we'll adopt. Get started right away."

She nodded her approval. Any other day she would have smiled. But it's hard to do when you know you've got to pack again. And that before long . . . written on a box . . . stashed in an obscure closet . . . you'd find these words:

"Contents: one baby blanket . . . blue."

PART IV

A Time to Gather Stones Together

This is part of the infinite goodness of God, that he should allow evil to exist, and out of it produce good.

Thomas Aquinas, *Summa Theologica*, First Part, Q2, Art. 3.

25

The Song Said It Best

Light from the rose window fell softly on the little casket. The chapel: packed with friends who felt a common bond of sadness. The organ prelude: the beginning of a substantial happening . . . one in which deep, spiritual transactions took place.

The scripture brought hope: Death is a start, not a finish. Quite a switch! We'd seen Angela's dying as a grand finale . . . for her . . . and for us.

With the sermon came a sense of strength. Something else we'd missed because we had our eyes closed.

The song said it best "How Firm a Foundation" . . . the sturdy American tune. Echoing the voices of pioneers in log churches overcoming tremendous hardship on the new frontier.

"What more can he say than to you he hath said . . . ?"
In so many ways we'd received the message.
"When through fiery trials thy pathway shall lie;
My grace all sufficient shall be thy supply."

We believed it.

"That soul, tho' all hell should endeavor to shake,
I'll never, no never, no never forsake."

The music caught us up, lifting, strengthening, reassuring. Words struck responsive chords within us. Sometimes tears choked our voices, but we felt a sense of grim determination, growing stronger as we sang. I gripped her hand a little tighter. This time we would overcome. No bitterness, no self-pity. Only grief. We could handle that.

26

He Never Knew

Ray Jordan had a lot to give. Great preacher, outstanding educator, noted author, Christian gentleman. For years, professor of homiletics at Candler School of Theology. Time and again I (and my campus colleagues) felt the sting of his red pencil—correcting, criticizing, teaching.

On the day after Michael's birth Ray Jordan suffered a heart attack. He and Vermelle were neighbors in intensive care although they never met.

When I'd visit her, I'd see his heartbeat, monitored on a machine outside his door. One day the device was gone. Ray Jordan had died.

I told Vermelle. She startled me with her response.

"Why?

". . . Why?

". . . . . . He did so much, lived such a productive life, helped so many people, had a deep and abiding faith . . . and yet he died. I cursed God and he let me live. There's got to be a reason. He spared me for a purpose. I know he did. I'll live to find it."

Purpose lit a fire that the darkness of Michael's death could not extinguish.

". . . I'll live to find it."

A bell tone ringing true and sweet across the valley of the shadow of death. He never knew how much he did for us. In his dying he helped Vermelle discover life.

27
Pick Them Up

During our terrible times we needed friends who could help in three ways:
1. By picking us up.
2. By pushing us off.
3. By keeping us going until we regained balance.

We found it comforting to know that people cared.

Precisely when our spiritual, physical, mental, and emotional bank accounts seemed overdrawn, we borrowed on the reserves of others. They came to cook, clean or whatever. The pick-them-up people found varieties of ways to show concern.

Telephone calls from acquaintances in other cities who had heard the news.

"Just calling to say we're thinking of you."

And from our home congregation . . . friends who'd been with us at the death of Angela.

"We're having a twenty-four-hour prayer vigil in your behalf. Thought you'd like to know."

Their faith in God called us back to ours.

Visits from neighbors. Some rode miles, others walked from next door. But most important, they came.

Telegrams . . . cards . . . letters. Expressing the deepest feelings of the sender. We appreciated every one.

Suddenly we realized the tremendous price we'd paid for bitterness. By choosing isolation, we had shut the gate on one of grief's great blessings—the expressions of love that others send our way. At no other point in life do people so openly offer their support.

It may be "more blessed to give," but there comes a time in every life when it's mighty pleasant to receive.

28

Push Them Off

Tender loving care is nice, but not as a steady diet. Sooner or later the best help comes from the "push-them-offers." They're the saints who recognize the value of a firm push (or a swift kick) into the mainstream of life. I count them high on my list of people for whom to be thankful.

I'll never forget the professor who understood the importance of a loving shove. I'd come back to school after a two-week absence . . . during which time Michael came and went. He saw me on that first day and called me aside. Didn't know what to expect.

"Mr. Bailey, we're having a test on Friday. You've missed a lot of time. I'm heartbroken over the death of your son."

I knew he cared because he'd come with the others to "pick us up." His manner reflected his concern. He continued.

"But even in the midst of turmoil it's important to keep our objectivity. I'd like to help you with this test. Give you more time to study . . . take the grade into consideration. But, I can't. You'll have to live with what you earn. I'm sorry, but I think it's best."

Cruel? No. I needed it. Helped me get up and go.

FOR EVERYTHING A SEASON

When the dust cleared, I had a C+. He apologized . . . said he wished I could have done better. But the warm twinkle in his eye said, "Now you're on your feet. Keep going."

29
Keep Them Going

Tragedy's initial blow brings with it a flurry of activity followed by an oppressing loneliness. Even best friends are busy and move on to other things. And yet, there are some in a class by themselves. They go the second mile. Not only are they present at the "pick-them-up" parties, they stick around to "keep-them-going." Not with major efforts, but with continued presence, and in less dramatic ways.

A phone call . . . the offer of a ride to town . . . or "Would you like to come for supper?" Sometimes they stopped by in passing, though only for a moment. Regardless of how they operated, we got the picture: "Anytime you have a problem, I'll be glad to help."

You appreciate friends like those. They're the ones who pull you through the mire of the dull days when the sharp pain becomes a throbbing ache.

But there's another type of super-helper. They had no idea where the Baileys were. To them location made no difference. In our case, "keeping going" meant overcoming a financial crisis in addition to the problems of grief.

Question: "How do you pay a hospital bill when it's more than half your year's salary?"

Answer: There were those who anticipated our need before it ever happened. They planned for us.

Went to the hospital one day to work out monthly installments. The financial officer pulled our records and socked me with the biggest surprise of my life.

"Sir, it's already taken care of."

"No. There must be some mistake."

No mistake. A wealthy doctor left a large portion of his estate for just such a purpose.

On another day I made my way to school oppressed by other bills that had accumulated while Vermelle was out of work. A staff member from the student affairs office met me in the hall.

"Ralph, I've a check for you. Know you've had lots of expenses. A friend of the school sent a donation to be used for assistance. Hope you can use it."

Could I ever! Cautiously, I looked—three hundred dollars.

All around us—people . . . some we'd never even met . . . who care enough to find a tangible way of saying, "I'm sorry."

30
The Gift from Mrs. Brown

Mrs. Brown's front yard would never win the "Garden of the Month Award" . . . unless they gave a prize for desolation. No grass. No shrubbery. Nothing, except for one chinaberry tree, and all its leaves had fallen weeks ago. The rusty remains of a defunct automobile cluttered what should have been the lawn. Wheelless—symbol of the despair its owner felt.

Several chickens pecked at the frozen ground . . . a lost cause . . . and a few more nested in the front seat's torn upholstery. December wind whipped across the countryside and whistled through the leafless tree, driving its way through broken window panes and into the rundown house that Mrs. Brown called home.

When your husband is in prison and you have five children . . . and a sixth on the way . . . you get along as best you can. In the case of Mrs. Brown, "as best you can" came nowhere near being good enough.

We climbed decaying steps, crossed the rotten porch,

and knocked. With a wrenching sigh, the door opened, just wide enough to let a pair of knee-high eyes look out. Warm air rushed to greet us, bringing with it the scent of wood smoke and human odors. I fought to keep my dinner down —but at least I had had a dinner.

"Your mother home?" I asked the eyes.

"Uh-huh."

From somewhere in the back . . . an adult voice.

"Who is it, Janie?"

"A man and a lady, Ma."

"Tell 'em to come in."

The room: unpainted . . . making the dim light less effective. Sparsely furnished with someone's attic rejects. Cardboard replaced at least a few of the broken windows— poor substitute for the real thing.

Mrs. Brown lay on a saggy bed, covered with a quilt. Sick, obviously pregnant. She never said a word of greeting, but her eyes asked, "What are you doing here?" I hardly knew the answer.

"Mrs. Brown . . . I came because I need your help."

She looked us over suspiciously, wondering what kind of scheme we'd planned. She'd been taken too many times by folks with special offers and free gifts. Her thoughts seemed far away . . . maybe with her husband in his cell. Wishing he were here to deal with us, loving him, missing him, at the same time hating him for leaving her alone, and for making her pregnant again. Her voice: weak and distant.

"You can see there ain't no way for me to help nobody."

"You can help us, Mrs. Brown. Our baby died three weeks ago. We'd planned a big Christmas . . . but without him it's not the same. You'd be helping if you'd let us buy some gifts for yours. We heard about Mr. Brown . . . and

THE GIFT FROM MRS. BROWN

it seemed . . . well . . . it just seemed like maybe we could get together"
"You had a son . . . he died," she said flatly.
"Yes."
"You wanted him bad?"
"More than I could ever tell you."
"Ain't that a hell of a note!" Shaking her head in disbelief. "You want children so much and don't have one. I got them running all over the place . . . wish to hell I didn't have to give birth to this one. I'da had an abortion if I knew where to go. When I get to the hospital, I'm gonna have an operation. Make damn sure it don't happen again."

Mrs. Brown symbolized everything we'd hated since Angela died. Unwanted children, disinterest in her unborn child, the whole package of conditions we abhorred.

I clenched my first, expecting I'd have to keep myself from hitting her. The rage never came. Instead I felt it drain away to be replaced by sympathy. Mrs. Brown had a problem, worse than any we had ever faced. I wanted to reach out, touch her, offer hope. To say I understood . . . as much as a person from my world can understand someone from hers. Realizing, in that moment, I could never really know her personal hell unless I lived in it. Found myself speechless.

On Christmas Eve we brought the presents. I never will forget the faces. Some party! But the gift from Mrs. Brown was the greatest of them all. She showed me that I'd hated because I didn't understand, helped me see how our "solutions" could be another couple's "problems." Took away my chains and set me free to love. Mrs. Brown salvaged Christmas and helped me find more of its real meaning than I'd ever known.

PART V

A Time to Seek

Poor Fletch. Don't believe what your eyes are telling you. All they show is limitations. Look with your understanding, find out what you already know, and you'll see the way to fly.

Richard Bach, *Jonathan Livingston Seagull*. (New York: The Macmillan Company, 1970), p. 92.

31

Move Out!

"Move out!"

Hate to hear it. Always will. Too often it means moving from certainty to uncertainty, from security to insecurity, from the known to the unknown, from the familiar to the unfamiliar. For us, on the way through the grief process, it meant a change of role . . . from a "cared for" to a "caring" person.

Frightening switch . . . complicated by a haunting fear: "Can I endure the threat of the free world after the warmth of protective custody?"

One young lady knew the problem. She'd recently returned from a retreat in Colorado. In the easy atmosphere she neatly packaged her beliefs. At home, in the old environment, assurance vanished. Here's what she said:

"The fellowship was fantastic. Around a campfire . . . in a friendship circle . . . watching sunsets in the peaks . . . I felt so sure of myself. Had every facet of my faith in place."

For a moment thoughts trailed off . . . remembering distant days on mountain tops.

"Now I'm a long way from Colorado."

How true! Hardly get beyond the gate before our armor starts to rust. Makes us want to hide outside the line of fire. But sooner or later, we all get re-called to active duty. Behind us: all we've ever known. Before us: a giant question mark.

Temptation: drop everything and run for cover. But the price for a permanent location is greater than the fear of leaving. Too long in one place and we begin to die. Memories have a way of fading. By boxing yesterday's shadows we lose the power to wrestle with today's realities. Dead flowers from the past can't hold a candle to petunias alive and well in your backyard.

"Move out!" The order of the day.

Facing life . . . and maybe being hurt again.

Head-on confrontation with tomorrow. The nose cone on a rocket lifting off for outer space.

Risking.

Vulnerable. But moving . . . because we can't afford to stay.

32
Everywhere I Go ... There I Am

Sunday afternoon. The bleachers ... crowded.
Standing amidst the throng ... a drunk. Bottle in one hand, glass in the other. In his best oratorical style, announcing a profound truth:
"Everywhere I go ... there I am."
Then he collapses.
"Everywhere I go ... there I am."
We can deny it, ignore it, pretend we didn't hear. But to no avail—because it's true. For him ... for us ... for all mankind.
We play the game of life in different arenas. But there is one standard rule:
"Everywhere I go ... there I am."
Fact: Before making peace with the world, we have to sign a treaty with ourselves. Sobering.
Our boozing buddy said it loud and clear:
"I'd rather face the darkness than the light."
Play it again, Sam ... play it again.

33

Balm in Gilead

"There is a balm in Gilead, to make the wounded whole."

Wise words from an old spiritual. I found my Gilead in the small group. Personal sharing, open and honest, releases healing power. But the "balm" bottle is corked with fear.

"Suppose I tell too much?"

"If my real identity shows . . . would they still care for me?"

"Can I trust them?"

"Will my private thoughts, shared confidentially, make headlines on the community grape vine?"

I waded in . . . a little at a time. Testing every step. Making the final plunge. Once immersed, I found the water refreshing.

Worth the risk? I think so.

The first benefit: a start toward self-acceptance. Even with its flaws, the "Ralph in hiding" looked better than the phony face that showed.

Then I began to untangle the strands of my knotty life. Identifying problems is the first step to dealing realistically with them.

In the warmth of a caring fellowship, I unlearned all society had taught concerning feelings:

"Keep smiling, no matter what."

"Big boys don't cry."

"I'd rather not get involved . . ."

And I learned to receive the gifts that others gave. Some accomplishment for a person who cut his teeth believing that self-giving was the only way to help.

We plumbed the depths of inner space and shared our findings. Moved on to new life. Enjoyed an exciting sense of freedom.

Affirming the positive.

Accepting limitations.

Admitting the existence of huge chunks of personality about which we still had a lot to learn.

Enjoying the support and encouragement that helped me glimpse the possibility of God's all-encompassing love.

34

Saw It on TV

Saw it on TV. Boxers . . . mentally and physically prepared. Punching . . . dodging . . . dancing. Each looking for the precise moment when he could smash his way to victory. Rolling with the punches. Getting hit, but—for the most part—avoiding full impact of the blow.

While pondering the making of a champion, I stumbled on some helpful hints for weathering a storm. Wish I'd found them long ago.

1. Flexibility increases odds for survival. Rigid people break under stress. Inflexibility limits our response to God's love. He works with us—even in agonizing times—creating, making all things new . . . if we relax enough to let him.

2. Preparation makes a difference. The fellows on TV trained hard *before* the bout. Hundreds of strenuous workouts.

We never give a thought to tragedy until the blows begin to fall. Then we wonder why the knockout comes.

3. A sense of balance is important. Makes for quick recoveries when the athlete is tipped off center.

Our stability comes with this affirmation: God is in crisis, wanting wholeness for us even as we seek it for ourselves.

4. It helps to be a student of the game. A boxer studies his opponent. Learns from his own mistakes and picks up techniques from others.

We make mistakes, but we aren't alone in our troubles. The world is full of burdened people making right and wrong decisions. There are living lessons all around us . . . if we open our eyes.

5. Crucial factor: the will to win. Can't get along without it. The real competitor hangs on with every ounce of energy. Battling back until he gains the prize.

Losing sight of life's goal sends us to the canvas for the count. In the middle of turmoil, reasons for existing can be hard to find. That's why training takes place before rather than during the main event.

Fight over; the announcer takes us to the dressing rooms for postmatch interviews. Even the loser has a word of wisdom:

"I think I could have won. He just surprised me with a good left. Next time I'll train a little different. Then I'll get him in the rematch."

Even in defeat . . . moving ahead to "next time." Analyzing, correcting, getting back in shape. He leaves the spotlights of the ring, away from the applause of those who cheer him. Heads for the isolation of a musty training camp . . . and starts all over.

We, too, can make the most of our "second shots" . . . if we learn from the ones we lose.

35
After Ten Years... Why?

"Why?"

After ten years, no answer. But an affirmation. "God constantly works to redeem our struggles. When trouble comes, "Why?" is no longer the primary question. But, "How?" How will God bring something creative from the chaos that surrounds us?

Angela triggered a chain reaction of attitudes and events. Consider:

1. She influenced my career.

A reassessment of our value system pointed me toward the ministry. Old patterns were so deeply ingrained, nothing short of personal tragedy could have broken the mold.

2. She strengthened our faith.

Forcing us to develop a more workable system of belief ... or discard it all together.

3. In her death she gave life.

Literally. I'll never forget the words of the doctor on the

AFTER TEN YEARS ... WHY?

terrible night we rushed Vermelle to the Emory University Hospital: "Two more minutes ... and she'd have died."

Two minutes. The margin between survival and oblivion. Going to seminary saved her by putting us in close proximity to the major hospital.

4. Through our tribulation we developed a deeper sense of togetherness. Foolishly, we thought we knew each other well. Facing hardship helped our marriage.

5. We adopted two wonderful children. Can't conceive of life without them. We believe they are a part of God's plan for us, and we for them.

6. We learned to hang on.

Jacob wrestled all night with the angel. In the morning he walked off ... with a limp. A souvenir of his encounter. But he also had a blessing. So did we.

7. We have a lifetime membership in the fellowship of sufferers. A special gift that comes with grief. An identity that opens doors to others in time of sorrow.

"Why?"

No answer. And yet, so much positive and good happened because of Angela and Michael. We affirm the hand of God, guiding and directing the pattern of our lives.

36
A Not So Gentle Reminder

Pueblo Nuevo: a small Costa Rican frontier town with one unique feature—a marvelous view. The city fathers had the inspiration to line their main street on lovely Mt. Aranal. Beautiful sight . . . tragic mistake. One August morning, the inactive volcano—the landscape's centerpiece—erupted in their faces, killing every person.

A year after the disaster, I visited the ruins. A not so gentle reminder of the desolate days when the landmarks of my own life blew up leaving me in despair.

The wind swept down the slopes . . . raced across the plain . . . singing in my ears: "Remember, Ralph . . . remember."

It's easy to forget the storms of yesterday in the present's peace and quiet. But in an instant it all came crashing home. Angela and Michael—the pain, the sorrow, the brokenness, the burden of my own mortality. Grim images from the past.

A NOT SO GENTLE REMINDER

Mt. Aranal stuck a finger of smoke in my face and seemed to ask a question:

"Have you, so soon, forgotten?"

I had. And now I stood, facing the awesome power of the mountain, feeling my own weakness. Reminded of the need for a life force greater than my own.

Thoughts turned to another hill . . . a place called Calvary. Symbol of God's ability to bring victory from defeat.

It's good we lose the past in mental mists. Dwelling on it makes us sick. But, it's a shame we overlook our source of strength when all is going well.

I needed a not so gentle reminder. In the rubble of a broken town, I found it.

37

The New Moses

"Keep looking. One day . . . in the bullrushes . . . you may find a new Moses." Voice of comfort at the time of Michael's death.

We looked . . . there they were . . . found two. We call them Kathy and Bill. Lovely people. Wish you could meet them.

The day each came to live with us is special. Red letter . . . filled with joy. And both times we heard the words again: "One day . . . in the bullrushes . . . you may find a new Moses."

When Kathy—she's ten—puts her arms around my neck . . . gives that special look that means, "Daddy, I love you" . . . well, right then I know I'm through hunting.

And when Bill—he's seven—climbs up in my lap with book in hand and asks those questions only he can fabricate, I'm sure we've found what we were searching for.

No doubt, you'll want to add a note of caution:

'Don't expect too much. Kids can only be themselves."

THE NEW MOSES

You're right. Dare not overburden them with our load of hope. They'll have to hammer out their patterns. Wander through mazes that they choose . . . and fall into some others which they didn't. May get lost and never find their way . . . who knows? Still, I'm convinced . . . we found our Moses. At least they've brought us from the wilderness . . . and led us to the promised land.

38

A Strong Hand and a Little Light

Overhead . . . a canopy of sprawling limbs. Moss, doing an eerie dance in the night breeze. The moon casting weird patterns on the path. Every sound a threat. Chill bumps rising on my neck. I gripped my father's hand more firmly.

"Daddy . . . I'm afraid of the dark."

We stopped.

"Now, son, show me what's scaring you."

"Over there . . . see it moving?"

Patiently, he'd shine his flashlight . . . make a shadow disappear.

"Look . . . by the fence."

A bush . . . and with his help I saw the creatures of the night for what they were. A strong hand and a little light worked wonders.

I'll be traveling other paths · . . sometimes alone. The future is uncertain. I'm wondering if tomorrow will re-

A STRONG HAND AND A LITTLE LIGHT

semble yesterday . . . hoping that it won't. Because I've felt a strong hand, seen a little light, I willingly step forward.

I'll see some new sights on the road. Sometimes I'll question, "Can I handle this?" Probably—if along the way I find a strong hand and a little light.

I remember learning how to swim. Churned the water with my frantic effort. Exhausted myself . . . and got nowhere. Later I learned to relax, work less, stay afloat longer. Never became the master of the sea, but I kept myself from going under. Hope the same principles apply to living.

I'd like to have a measure of freedom. Find courage to move away from my protective shell, to accept the hurts that come with being vulnerable.

The Psalmist found the faith for which I'm looking:

"Even when walking through the dark valley of death, I will not be afraid, for you are close beside me, guarding, guiding all the way." [*]

I will make it . . . know I can . . . if only there's a strong hand and a little light.

---

[*] Psalm 23:4, *The Living Bible*. (Wheaton, Ill.: Tyndale House, Publishers, 1971), p. 453.

39

Last Tag

Last tag: one of childhood's simple ceremonies.
After time well spent with friends, it seemed the thing to do. One last touch before you go. Run away, shouting, "Gottcha last tag."
An important moment . . . packed with meaning. It preserved the spirit of the day. Something warm to travel with you on the long walk home. In spite of being all alone, I'd smile, remembering all we'd shared. A guarantee: next time he'd try to last tag me . . . something to which to look forward.
It served another purpose. All days aren't so filled with fun and sunshine. After empty hours, "last tag" became a question:
"Is there a moment worth remembering?"
Maybe then I'd run a little slower—wanting to be touched, listening for the words "Last tag." Sounds to lend some substance to the nothingness I felt.

LAST TAG

I feel compelled to "last tag" you. Reaching out with fear and trembling. Recalling how *no* book met my need. So many times I read in desperation . . . and went away as empty as I came. Those hollow moments spurred me on. Inspired by the helpless days when nothing seems to fit. Still, I've tried to say it . . . and now I offer one last tag.

In August of 1940 a hurricane smashed into the South Carolina coast leaving devastation in its wake. I was three years old. Lightning . . . thunder . . . howling wind . . . torrential rain . . . and fear permanently etched into the fabric of my life. The river overflowed its banks to flood our house. We grabbed a few necessities and moved to higher ground—the second floor of an old cotton-gin house.

Our food supply soon disappeared when shared with others who had taken refuge there. After the worst was over, we evacuated. Roads: impassable . . . wharves: destroyed. A small rowboat provided the only means of escape.

Waves crashed against the sides and sprayed our faces Rain: stinging pellets driven by the wind. Visibility: near zero.

We had a strategy: Hug the marshy shoreline until the last possible minute (If we sank, we wouldn't have far to swim.) At precisely the right point, we'd make a break. Cross over to the village on the other shore.

To attempt it was an act of faith. Couldn't see where we were going . . . wondered how much longer we could stay afloat . . . thought we'd never get across.

Then, dead ahead . . . through the mist . . . a dark figure: a mighty oak, standing tall, and we'd made it safely.

In my mind, the tree has often been a symbol. When

FOR EVERYTHING A SEASON

other storms have threatened, I keep looking for the shore. Believing that if I hang on long enough, I'll see a sign that shelter can't be far away.

I came home to write this book. Sailboats skim the water now, and fishermen enjoy themselves along the banks. Sunshine sparkles on the ripples. Gulls soar overhead. Cool breeze from the sea brings with it sounds of distant surf. My friend the oak . . . still there . . . majestic . . . ruler of the point on which he stands. Inviting me to face the future . . . confident that every crisis has its "other side."

These things he said in words. But much in his heart remained unsaid. For he himself could not speak his deepest secret.

Kahlil Gibran, *The Prophet*. (New York: Alfred A. Knopf, 1969), p. 7.